I0798694

Masters of Technic

Level 1

Technic etudes with emphasis on melody

Compiled, edited and arranged by Jeff Schaum and Wesley Schaum

FOREWORD

Numerous concert pianists and teachers were famous for their insights and development of successful piano technic, particularly during the 1800's. This series of books gives students an exposure to the rich variety of this technic heritage along with the benefits.

Level One presents ten different master technic composers. Emphasis is placed on the ***melodic aspect of technic*** for greater student appeal. The exercises are purposely condensed, modified or transposed for this level. Equal hand development is attained by similar exercises alternately emphasizing right hand and left hand. Different key signatures, appropriate to Level One, give students experience in various hand positions with black keys.

Measure numbers in a small box are included at the beginning of each system of music. This makes it easier to locate measures during the lesson and for written practice assignments.

The exercises are arranged in order of increasing difficulty. While becoming more challenging, the exercises complement the progress in a method book at the same level.

See the Composer Index on page 24

PRACTICE SUGGESTIONS

To derive the most benefit, attention should be given to how the exercises are practiced. ***Careful listening*** is necessary in order to hear a good balance between the accompaniment and the melody. The accompaniment should not be too loud. It is also important to listen for steady and accurate rhythm, and to make sure each finger plays equally loud, especially the 4th and 5th fingers.

Each exercise should be practiced four or five times daily, starting at a slow tempo and gradually increasing the speed as proficiency improves. Several previously learned exercises should be reviewed each week as part of regular practice.

Schaum Publications, Inc.
10235 N. Port Washington Rd. • Mequon, WI 53092
www.schaumpiano.net

04-41
KH-3

Wolff - C major 5-finger etude

Allegro ♩= 112-126

Op. 130, No. 1

Wolff - G major 5-finger etude

Allegro ♩= 112-126

Op. 130, No. 2

Mana-Zucca - Alternating hand positions

Allegro ♩= 116-132

Op. Posth.

Berens - F major 2-note phrase groups*

Vivace ♩= 138-160

Op. 70, No. 7

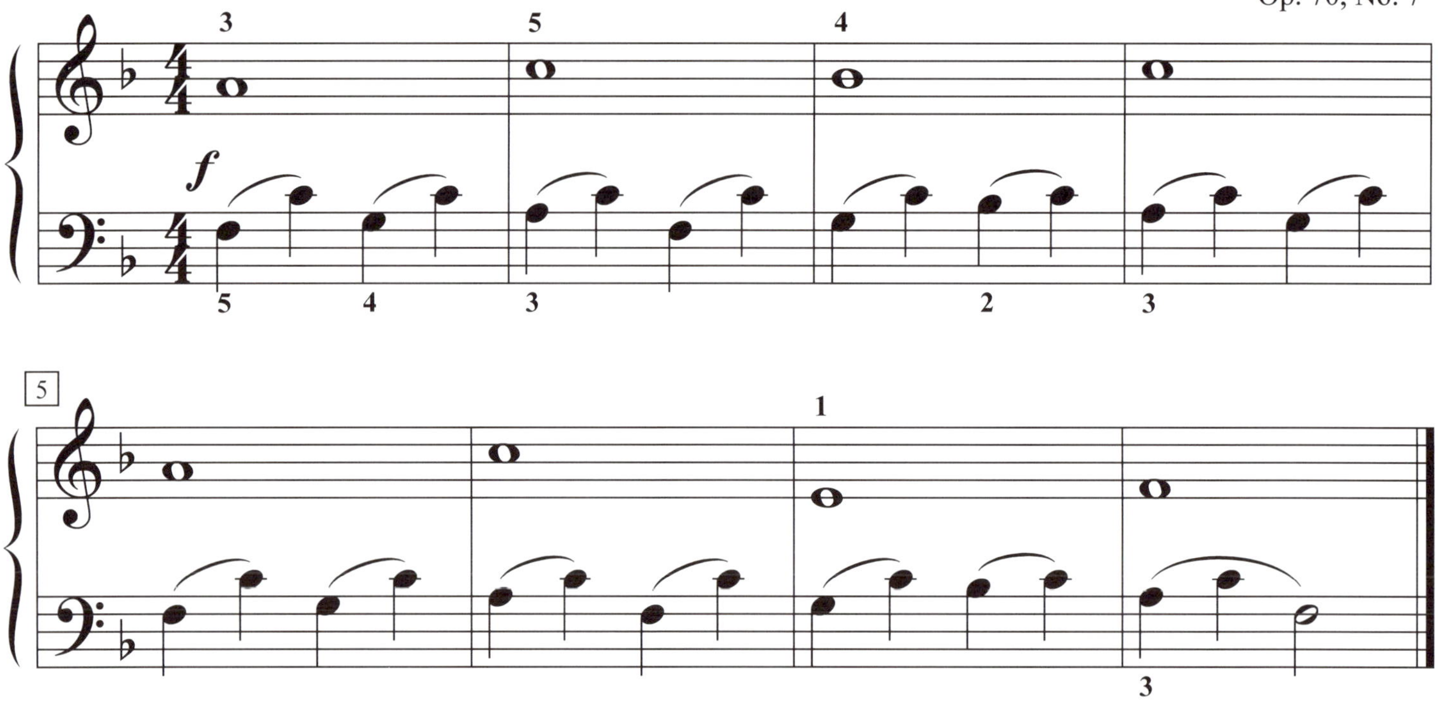

Berens - C major 2-note phrase groups

Vivace ♩= 138-160

Op. 70, No. 7

* Teacher's Note: Phrase marks are used to indicate note groups that form a pattern. The student should be shown how to recognize the ***patterns that recur*** in the exercises on this page.

Mana-Zucca - Dynamic contrasts

Köhler - 2nds and 3rds in C major

Allegro ♩= 132-160

Op. 218, No. 9

Köhler - 2nds and 3rds in G major

Allegro ♩= 132-160

Op. 218, No. 9

Gurlitt - F major 5-finger legato

Allegretto ♩= 116-132

Op. 82, No. 10

Gurlitt - G major 5-finger legato

Allegretto ♩= 116-132

Op. 82, No. 11

Duvernoy - Expanded hand position with staccato

Vivace ♩= 132-152

Op. 176, No. 25

Loeschhorn - C major 5-finger etude

Moderato ♩= 104-116

Op. 84, No. 3

Loeschhorn - B-flat major 5-finger etude

Moderato ♩= 104-116

Op. 84, No. 3

Czerny - Right hand legato and staccato

Op. 139, No. 7

Allegretto ♩= 126-144

Hanon - Right hand expansion

Vivace ♩= 160-184

Virtuoso Pianist, No. 1

Hanon - Left hand expansion

Allegro ♩= 144-168

Virtuoso Pianist, No. 21

Czerny - G major hand independence

100 Recreations, No. 17

Moderato ♩ = 96-112

Köhler - C major hand expansion

Allegretto ♩= 120-138

Op. 218, No. 26

Köhler - Parallel motion with 3rds and 6ths

Moderato ♩= 100-112

Op. 218, No. 18

Czerny - F major 5-finger pattern

Andante ♩= 92-108

Op. 599, No. 12

Gurlitt - Expanded 5-finger position

Op. 83, No. 13

Andante ♩ = 80-96

Loeschhorn - D major interval etude

Animato ♩= 108-126 Op. 84, No. 1

Loeschhorn - B-flat major interval etude

Animato ♩= 108-126 Op. 84, No. 1

Wolff - D major 5-finger trill patterns

Andante ♩= 76-92

Op. 130, No. 7

Andante ♩= 76-92 (This optional version is the same as above, but it is ***transposed*** to the key of G major.)

Biehl - B-flat major patterns with 3rds

Moderato ♩= 108-120

Op. 44, No. 4

Loeschhorn - *Hand position changes*

(Red circles indicate hand position changes.)

Andante ♩= 80-92

Op. 65, No. 4

Berens - Left hand melody with rotating accompaniment

Andantino ♩= 92-104

Op. 70, No. 11

Andantino ♩= 92-104

This is an optional version for extra study. It is the same as above, but it is ***transposed*** to the key of D major. Notice that the ***fingering is the same*** in both versions.

Duvernoy - Thumb cross-overs with broken chord bass

Cantabile ♩ = 104-116

Op. 176, No. 3

Teacher's note: Phrase marks in the bass staff are intended to show patterns in the accompaniment. Point out to the student that many of these patterns are repeated.

Composer Index